I CAN HELP
Save
Water

KT-539-571

Viv Smith

W
FRANKLIN WATTS
LONDON•SYDNEY

LINCOLNSHIRE
COUNTY COUNCIL

First Published in 1999 by
Franklin Watts

Franklin Watts
96 Leonard Street
London EC2A 4XD

© Franklin Watts 1999

Franklin Watts Australia
56 O'Riordan Street
Alexandria, Sydney
NSW 2015

Editor: Helen Lanz
Art Director: Robert Walster
Designer: Sally Boothroyd
Environmental consultant: John Baines
Commissioned photography: Steve Shott
Illustrations: Kim Woolley

Printed in China

ISBN: 0 7496 4294 7
Dewey Decimal Number: 363.73
A CIP catalogue record for this book is
available from the British Library.

Picture Credits
Cover: Steve Shott
Interior pictures: Franklin Watts 5 br, 18 br, 19,
23 t, 29/Harry Cory-Wright 18 tl; Friends of
the Earth 13 bl/Jennifer Bates, 24/Dylan
Garcia, 25/Jonathan Rose; Still Pictures
8/DRA, 10/Mark Edwards, 14/Andre
Maslennikov; Thames Water Picture Library
16. All other interior images by Steve Shott.

The publishers would like to thank St
Leonard's Primary School, Stafford, for their
help and enthusiasm, especially Viv Smith
and Class 2S who feature in this series.

Thank you also to Still Pictures for
photographs supplied for this book.

Contents

Have a drink!

We use water for many things . . . cleaning, cooking, washing, and of course we need water to drink.

Water is also needed to make many of the things we use every day. The cup you drink tea from may be made of china – china is made from clay and water. The paper you write on at school is made from wood pulp and water.

Most types of drinks are made with water, even fizzy ones.

Three-quarters of your body is made up of water. You need to drink about 1,000 litres of water a year.

6

HAVE A GO!

Think carefully about all the things you use water for when you are at home. Remember to include what you eat and drink. Would your list be different in summer than in winter?

Much of the food we eat has water in it too. Some foods, like soup and jelly, need to have water added before we can eat them.

Things that I use water for

having a bath
making a drink of orange
washing my hair
making a cup of tea
watering my mum's plants
brushing my teeth
flushing the toilet

We cannot survive without water.

Where water comes from

Look at this photograph of the earth taken from space. Isn't it beautiful? The blue areas are seas and oceans. The white patches are clouds, which are made of water too.

FASCINATING FACT!

Nearly all the water on earth (97%) is in the seas and oceans and is too salty to drink.

The world looks blue from space because well over half of the world is covered in sea water.

We cannot drink sea water, but seas, oceans and clouds make up part of the water cycle.

The water cycle gives us the water that we use and drink.

The Water Cycle

2. The drops of water form clouds.

3. The water droplets get bigger and heavier. Then they fall as rain.

4. The rain falls and runs back into all the ponds, lakes, rivers and seas. The cycle begins again.

1. Water in ponds, lakes, rivers and the sea is heated up by the sun. It turns into drops of water in the air, or water vapour.

In spite of all the rain which spoils playtimes and holidays, we can still run out of water so we need to use it carefully.

✂ HAVE A GO!

Put a saucer of water on a sunny window-sill. Mark where the level of the water is with a waterproof pen. Check the saucer every day. Mark each new water-level. What do you notice?

The water we use

We use enormous amounts of water every day. Though there may seem to be a never-ending supply, it does not always rain at the right time or place, or in the amount that we need.

👀 **LOOK BACK**

Look back to pages 6 and 7. Remember the ways you used water at home?

We use lots of water to keep clean.

FASCINATING FACT!

Every person in Britain uses about 45,000 litres of water a year. That's about 5,000 bucketsful. You could probably fill your classroom with this.

HAVE A GO!

Use this list to help you check how much water your family uses in a day. These amounts may not be exactly right, but they will help to give you some idea.

ACTIVITY (per day)	AMOUNT OF WATER USED PER PERSON
Flushing toilet	9 litres
Having a bath	90 litres
Having a shower	30 litres
Dishwasher	55 litres per load
Washing up by hand	12 litres
Washing machine	118 litres per load
Garden sprinkler	10 litres per minute

Industry uses thousands of litres of water a day.

FASCINATING FACT!

Farmers need to use a lot of water, too. Did you know that a cow drinks about 135 litres of water a day?

Factories and power stations also use a lot of water every day. Water is used to make many different things. It is used to cool things down and heat them up.

IT TAKES ...	of water TO MAKE...
1 litre	100g chocolate bar
130 litres	bicycle
760,000 litres	four car tyres
9 litres	a newspaper
70 litres	4½ litres of petrol

Dirty water

Think of all the ways you can make water dirty at home. For example, by having a bath, washing clothes, washing the dishes, cleaning the car, using the toilet, cleaning your wellies or bathing the dog.

Water won't clean these different things by itself. What do you put into it to help?

Washing powders and washing-up liquids contain detergents. These are chemicals which we use to help us clean dirty things.

HAVE A GO!

You can see how detergents stick to both water and oil. Get a clear plastic bottle and pour water into it until it is about half full.

1 Carefully pour in a small amount of cooking-oil.

Now shake the bottle. What happens?

2 Now add some washing-up liquid. Shake the bottle again. What do you see?

Part of a detergent likes to attach itself to grease and the other part loves water. So the detergent makes the dirt and water stick together.

When we have finished washing, the detergent and dirty water go down the drain. So, as we keep clean, we make water dirty. Dirty water is a problem. It needs cleaning before we can use it again.

Sometimes dirty water gets into rivers and pollutes the fresh water.

13

Water pollution

Can you think of other ways that people make water dirty?

Farmers use a lot of fertilisers on their crops to make them grow. They also spray their crops with pesticides to stop them from being eaten by insects. Fertilisers and pesticides are chemicals.

LOOK BACK

Look back to page 12 to see how easy it is to make water dirty at home.

When crops are sprayed (left), some of the chemicals go onto the crops and some go onto the soil. From there, the chemicals can get into our water supply.

When crops are sprayed, chemicals can be blown by the wind into rivers.

1. Farmers spray fertilisers, pesticides and other chemicals onto their crops and the soil.

2. Rain falls.

3. Rain water runs over the soil into streams, carrying with it some of the chemicals.

4. Some water seeps into the soil to join water that collects below the ground.

stream

bore hole

5. The underground water can become polluted with the chemicals in the soil.

water seeps through rock

water absorbed (taken in) by rock

water cannot pass through rock

6. Some water (and chemicals) seep through the soil and into streams.

Below the ground, there is a store of water. This is rain water that has gone into the soil and collected underground. We use it for drinking (we collect it through bore holes). It is also used by plants. But chemicals, oil and detergents seep into the ground and can pollute this water.

We need to try to use less water, think about what we put into our water and keep our water clean.

FASCINATING FACT!

Pollution from cars and factories is released into the air. It mixes with water in clouds to make acid rain. When acid rain falls, it goes into lakes, river and seas. It can kill fish and other wildlife.

How water is cleaned

All the water that we drink and use in our homes is cleaned. Find out where your nearest water-treatment (sewage) works is and the name of your local water authority.

The less we put in to pollute water, the less the water authorities have to clean out.

 **HAVE A GO!**

Ask your teacher if someone from the local sewage-works or water authority can come in to your school to talk to you about what they do. You might even be able to visit them.

Water is tested to see how clean it is before it goes into our homes.

✂ HAVE A GO!

You can do an experiment to find out how water is cleaned. Ask an adult to help you collect some dirty water. Remember to wear rubber gloves.

1. Cut the top off a plastic bottle, turn the top upside down and place it in the body of the bottle like a funnel.

2.  Put kitchen paper, some gravel, and a layer of sand into the pot.

3. Slowly pour the dirty water into the funnel and wait for it to drip through.

Does the water that drips through look cleaner than it did before? Can you think why?

✳ WATCH OUT!

Always have an adult with you if you go near to ponds, lakes or streams.

This gives us an idea how water is cleaned. But the water we drink has to be cleaned much more than this.

✳ WATCH OUT!

The water is still dirty and will have germs in it. Don't put it near your mouth.

It is up to all of us to help to keep water clean and to reduce how much water we use.

17

Saving water

It is easy to waste water. It just runs away! But there are steps we can all take to help save water.

 **HAVE A GO!**

Do you leave the tap running while you clean your teeth? Next time you brush your teeth, put the plug in your wash basin. Let the water run until you have finished.

Scoop the water you have collected into a measuring jug. How much water was in the sink? Just think, if you had turned the tap off you would have saved all that water. Every little helps!

Almost half the water used in one day in the home goes on flushing the toilet. Every flush uses about 9 litres of water. Some modern toilets use half this amount.

To reduce the amount of water you use in each flush, fill a litre plastic bottle with water.
Get an adult to help you put it on its side in the cistern (the container at the top of the toilet), away from the ball-cock and valve.

Some water authorities give out 'hippo' bags (like the one to the left) to put in the toilet cistern.

◉◉ LOOK BACK

Look back to page 11 to see how much water a dishwasher uses for every load and how much you use if you wash up by hand.
Remember, even if you don't save much water, a dishwasher uses electricity, too.

If you have a dishwasher, how often is it used? How often would you wash up by hand if you didn't have one? You can help by making sure that the dishwasher is full every time it is switched on.

Recycling water

Have you heard of a hose-pipe ban? It means you cannot use a hose-pipe for watering the garden or washing the car. Usually, there is a hose-pipe ban when there has not been enough rain to replace the water we have used.

Why do you think it's bad to use hose-pipes when there has not been much rain?

FASCINATING FACT!

It takes about 30 litres of water to wash a car if you use two or three bucketsful of water. Spraying the car with a hose-pipe can use up to 9 litres of water a minute. This would mean using about 180 litres, if it took twenty minutes to do the job.

Cleaning the car by hand not only saves water but can also be fun if two of you do it.

Garden sprinklers use a lot of water – about 10 litres a minute. If you left a sprinkler on to water the grass for an hour, it would use about 600 litres of water.

It uses much less water if you water your plants with a watering-can. Why not recycle water from the washing-up or use rainwater that has collected in a water-butt?

If the weather is very hot and dry for a while, don't worry if the grass goes a bit brown. It will recover!

Be water-friendly!

How did you and your family keep clean today?
Did you have a bath or wash your
clothes? Perhaps you washed
your hair?

✂ HAVE A GO!

Ask an adult to help you
look in your bathroom and
kitchen for shampoos, soaps
washing-up liquids and
cleaning fluids.

Look at the labels to see if
you can find the word
'biodegradable'.

Cleaning products	bio.
soap	
shampoo	
bath cleaner	
washing up liquid	
oven cleaner	✓
washing powder	
bleach	✓

※ **WATCH OUT!**
Many cleaning fluids are harmful. Always have an adult with you. Wash your hands if you have touched the containers.

FASCINATING FACT!

Biodegradable means that something will rot down naturally.

When you go shopping, ask your family to buy 'environmentally-sensitive' cleaning fluids. These contain fewer chemicals. Also, the biodegradable chemicals that are used can be absorbed (taken in) by the earth more easily, and so do less damage.

Fresh and clean

It is important that we keep our water clean. Dirty water can affect our health and kill wildlife. It is up to all of us to help. It is not just the job of big organisations and governments.

Some problems seem so big that we may think there's nothing we can do about them. But there is.

LOOK BACK

Look back to the picture on page 8 and see how the oceans are connected together. Pollution which goes into one place can spread around the whole world.

If we look after our water supplies, we can continue to enjoy visiting beautiful places like this.

We can help to keep our rivers and lakes clean by making sure that we throw our litter away carefully.

We can use cleaning fluids that are more environmentally-sensitive and won't pollute the water as much as other fluids.

On short journeys, walk or cycle instead of going in the car. This cuts down on air pollution, which helps to stop acid rain.

Recycle water whenever possible. Plants are happy to drink rainwater from a water-butt, or washing-up water.

We all need to think carefully about how we use water every day. Think about how we can save water and help to keep it clean.

25

More activities and facts

✂ HAVE A GO!

Can you do any of the following things without using water?

- make a cup of tea
- wash your face
- go for a swim
- drink a can of fizzy cola
- clean your teeth
- make a jelly

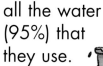

⚠ FASCINATING FACT!

Factories, mills and power stations use a lot of water each day. However, many places now recycle water. Most power stations recycle nearly all the water (95%) that they use.

✂ HAVE A GO!

Make a list of all the things you use water for at school. Think about the lessons you do and also what you do at playtime and lunchtime.

FASCINATING FACT!

People use up nearly half of the water which falls across the world.

HAVE A GO!

Try putting drops of water onto a large feather. What do you notice?

Birds put special oil from their bodies onto their feathers to help them keep dry and warm.

When thick oil escapes from a large ship and covers the seas, it clogs up seabirds' feathers. This stops them from being waterproof. The birds get cold and wet. Sometimes they die. Oil spills must be cleaned up carefully to protect wildlife and water systems.

LOOK BACK

Look back to page 15 to find out about acid rain. In Sweden, over 4,000 out of 85,000 lakes have no fish in them – the water is too acid.

FASCINATING FACT!

Acid rain can be caused by air pollution created in one country, that is blown by the wind across the globe into another country. Here the pollution mixes with rain clouds and falls as acid rain.

LOOK BACK

Look back to page 13 to see how oil floats on water. Natural oil on birds' feathers stops water from soaking into them.

Useful words

acid rain: rainfall that absorbs (takes in) the pollution from burning fuels like oil and coal. Acid rain can damage wildlife and buildings.

biodegradable: chemicals which rot down and do less harm to the environment.

bore hole: a hole that has been drilled into the ground. Page 15 describes a bore hole for reaching water below the ground.

chemicals: chemicals can be liquids, powders or gases that are mixed together to give certain reactions. Chemicals are used in fertilisers, pesticides and cleaning fluids.

detergent: chemicals for cleaning. Detergents are usually found in washing powders and washing-up liquids.

28

environment: the air, land and water where all plants, animals and people live.

environmentally-sensitive: a term used to describe chemicals or the things we do that cause less pollution and harm to the environment.

fertiliser: something that is added to the soil to make plants grow.

ocean: a very large sea.

pesticide: chemicals used to kill insects which eat plants and crops.

pollute: to make the land, air or water dirty.

power station: a building where electrical power is made.

seep: when something gradually leaks through or into something else.

sewage: water which contains waste products flushed down drains, sinks and toilets.

water authority: a company that cleans and supplies us with the water we use every day.

Index

30